On the Wall

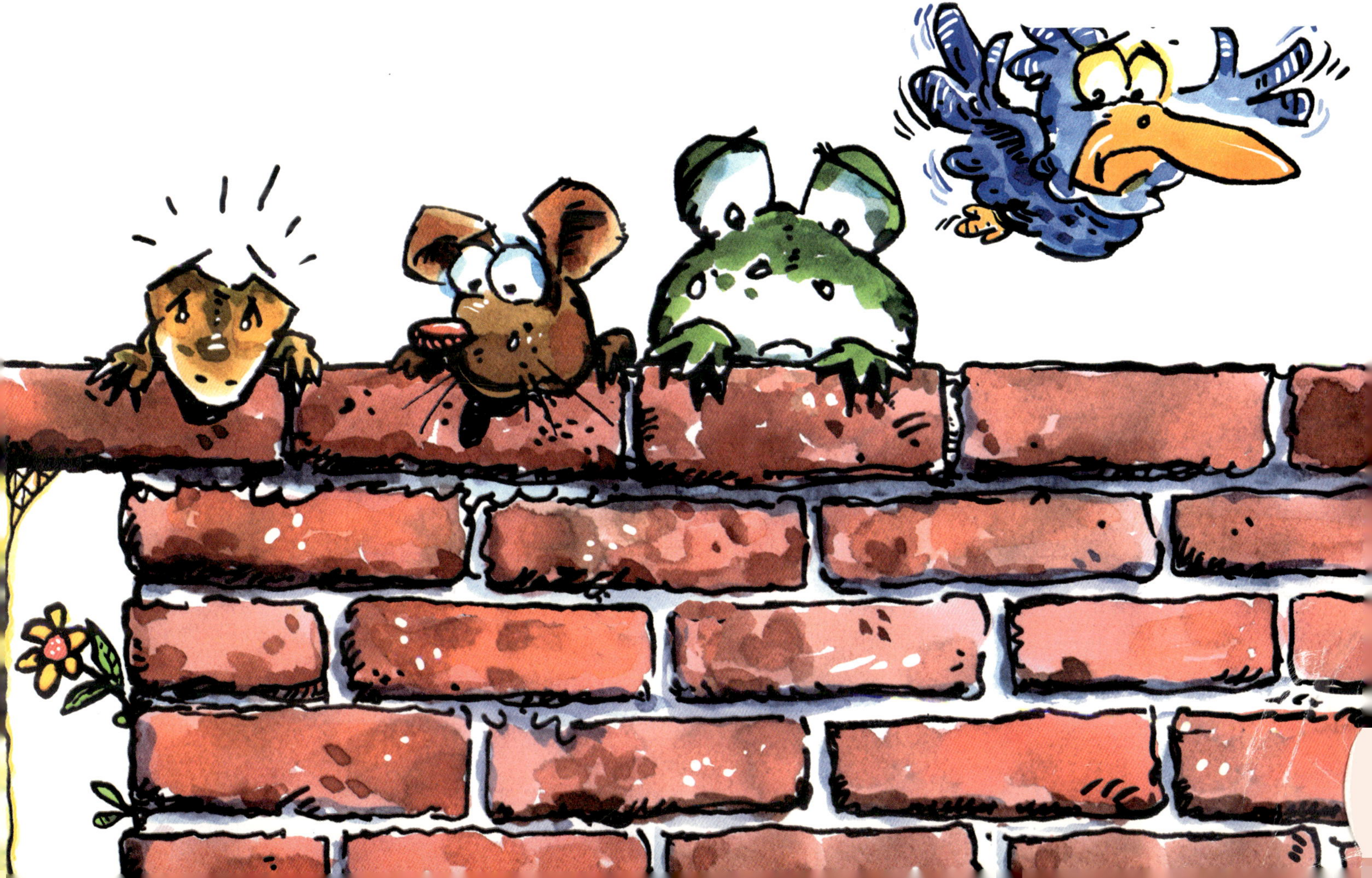

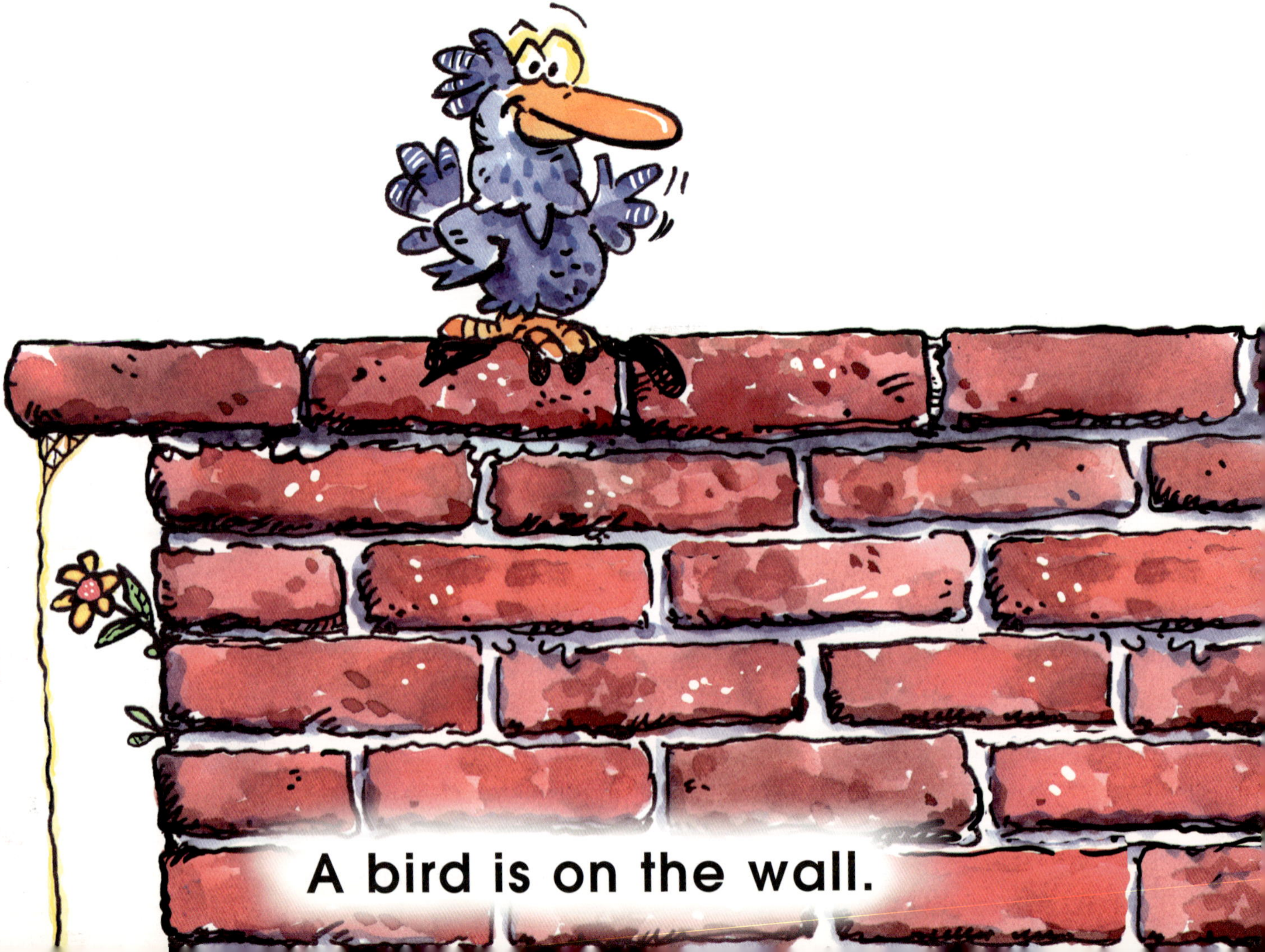

A bird is on the wall.

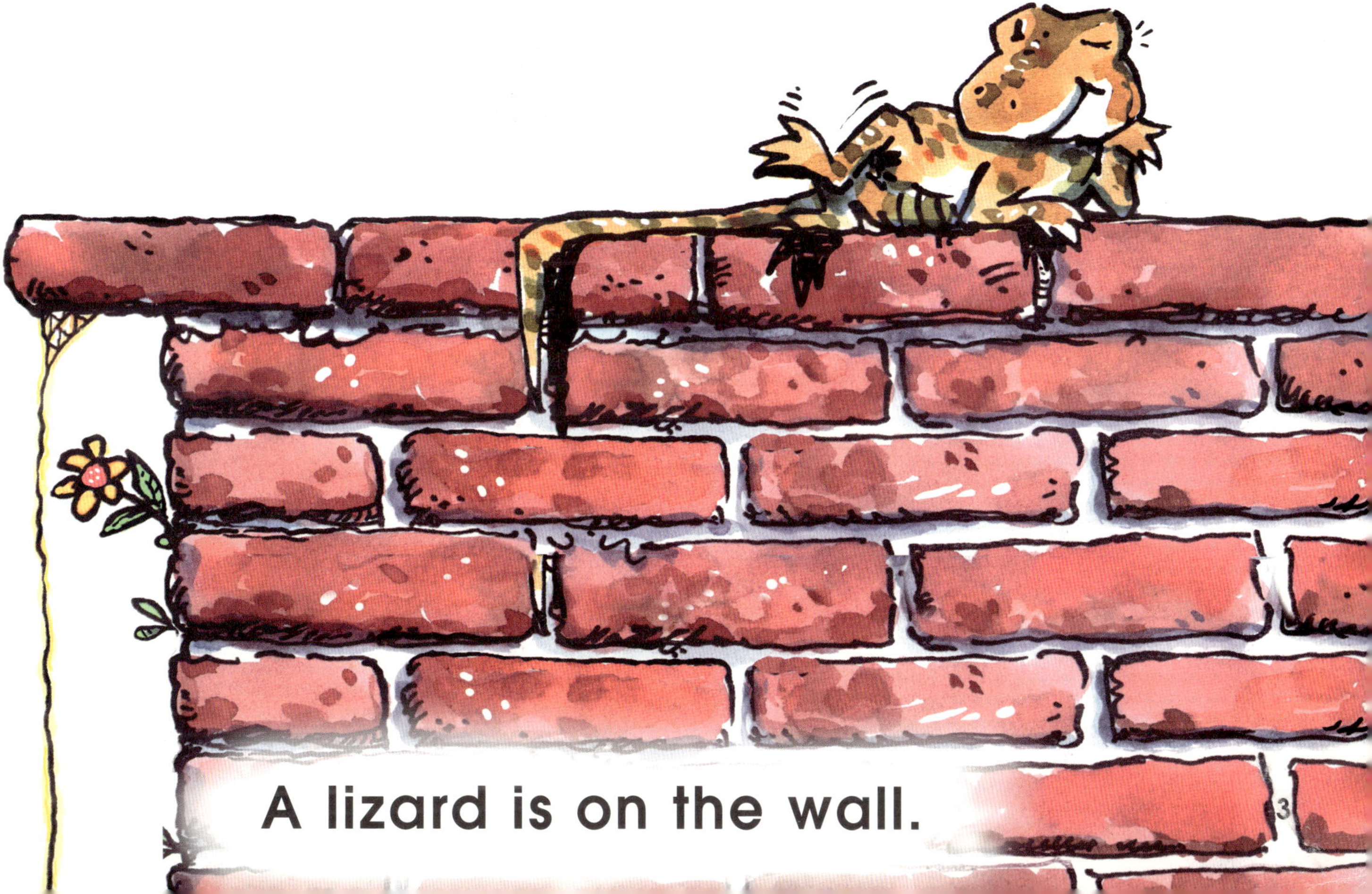

A lizard is on the wall.

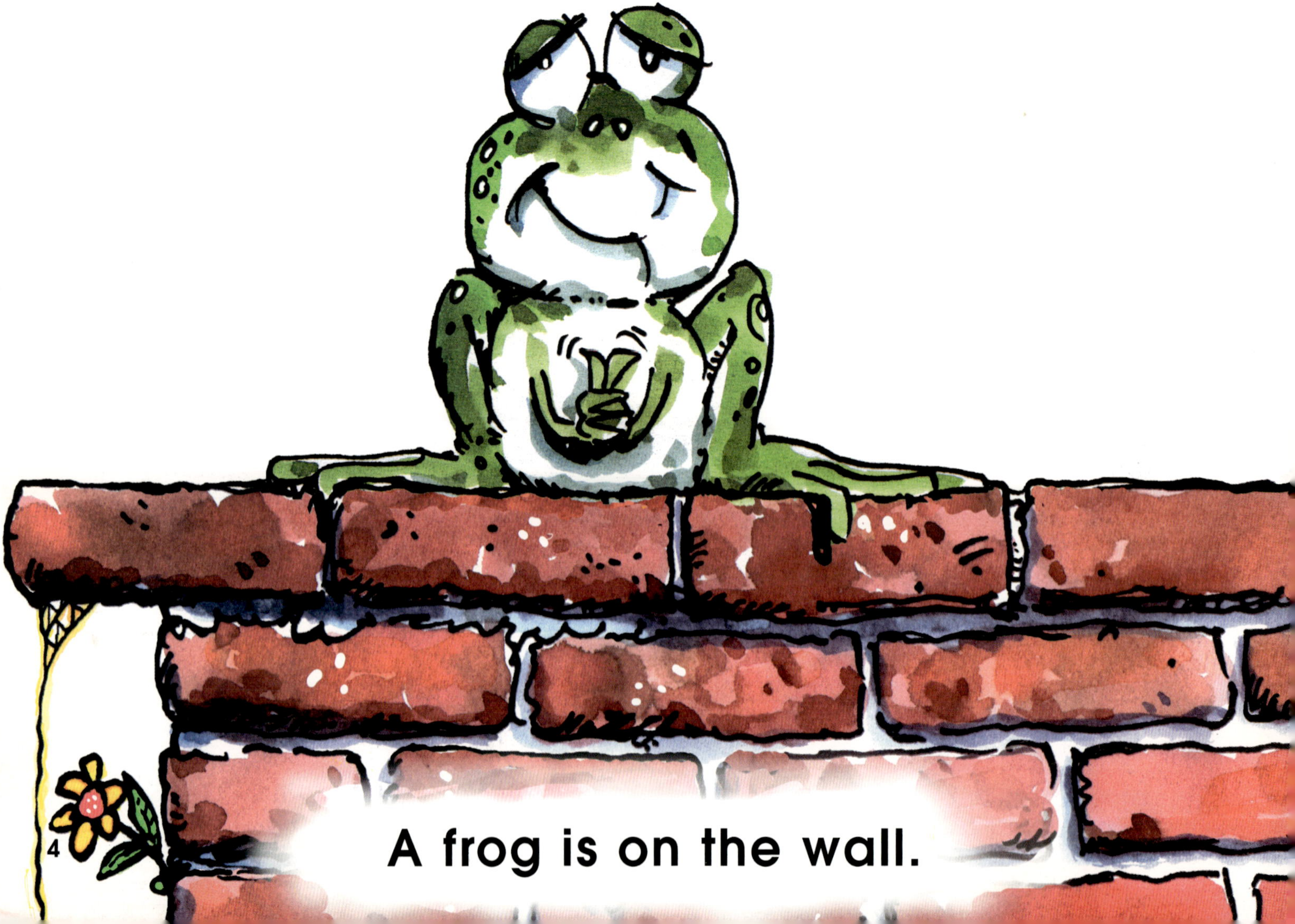

A frog is on the wall.

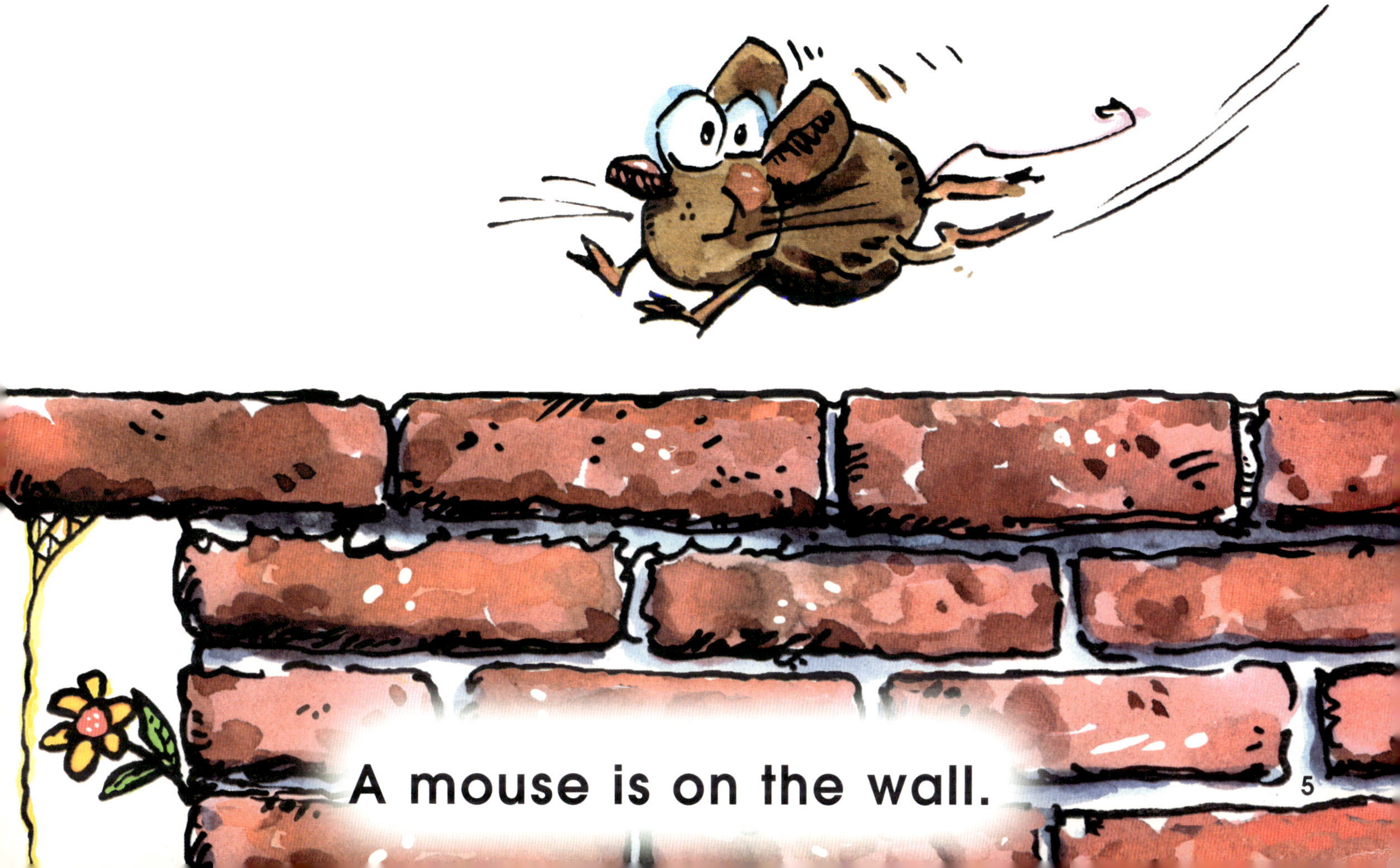

A mouse is on the wall.

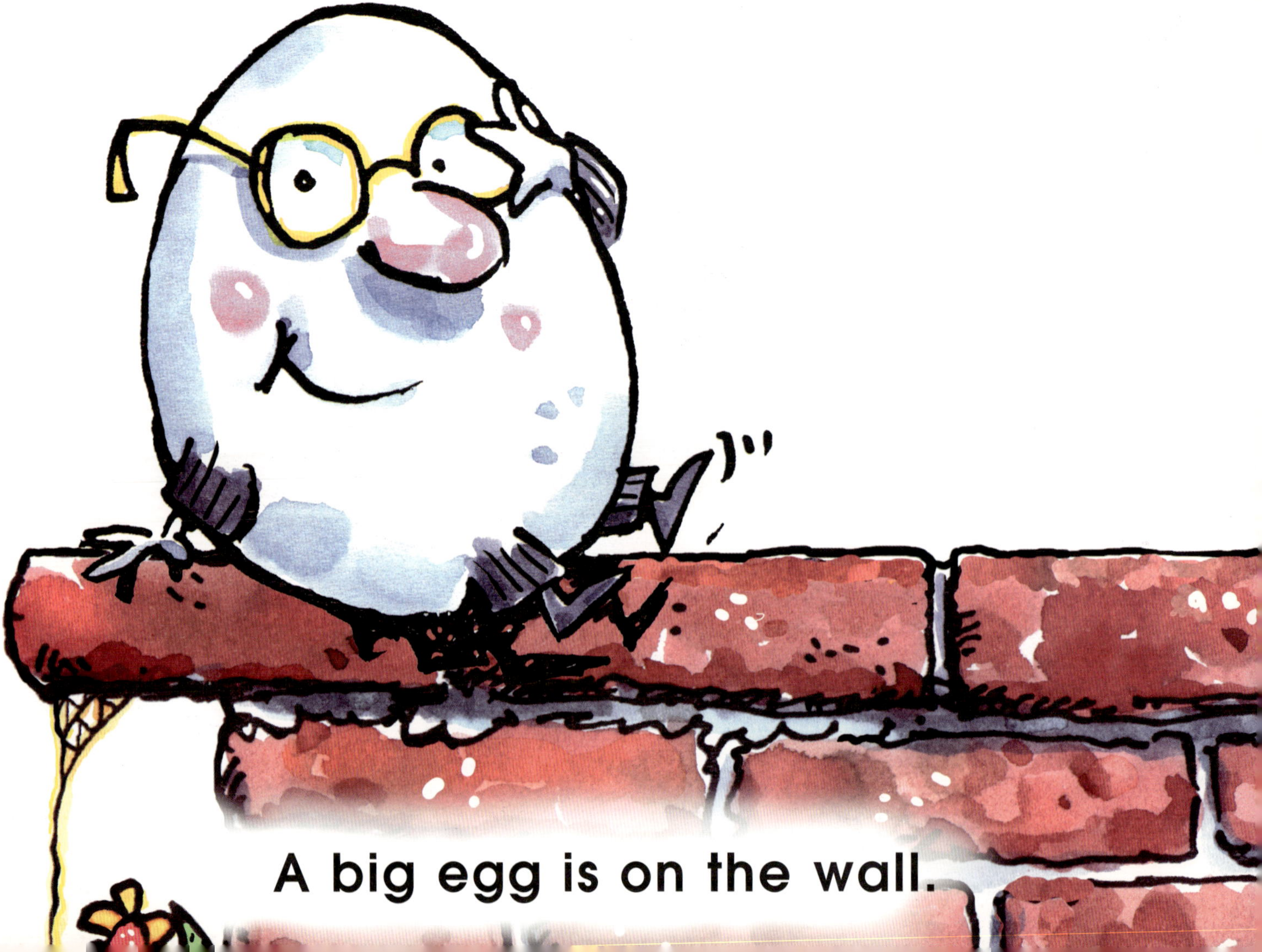

A big egg is on the wall.

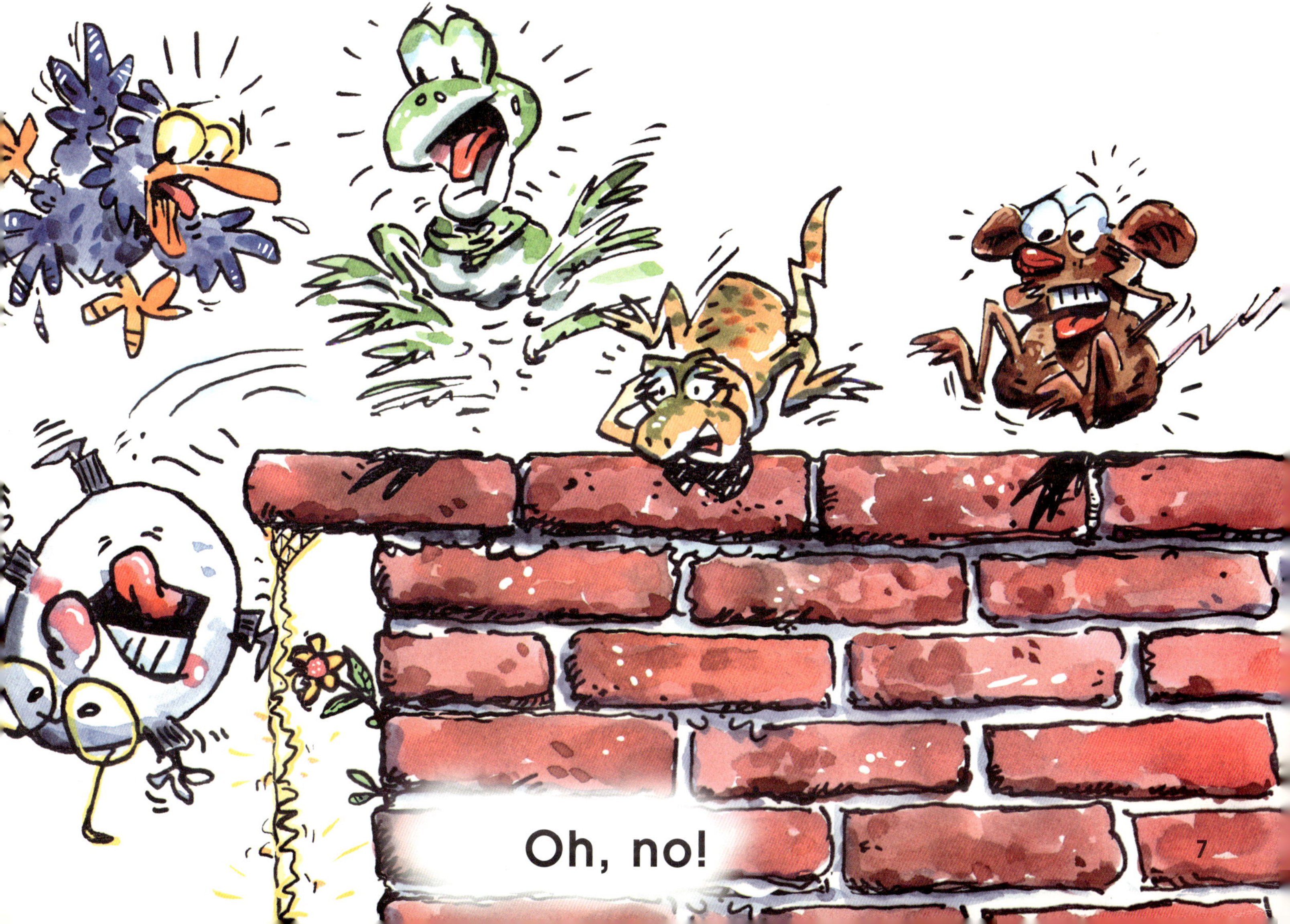

Oh, no!

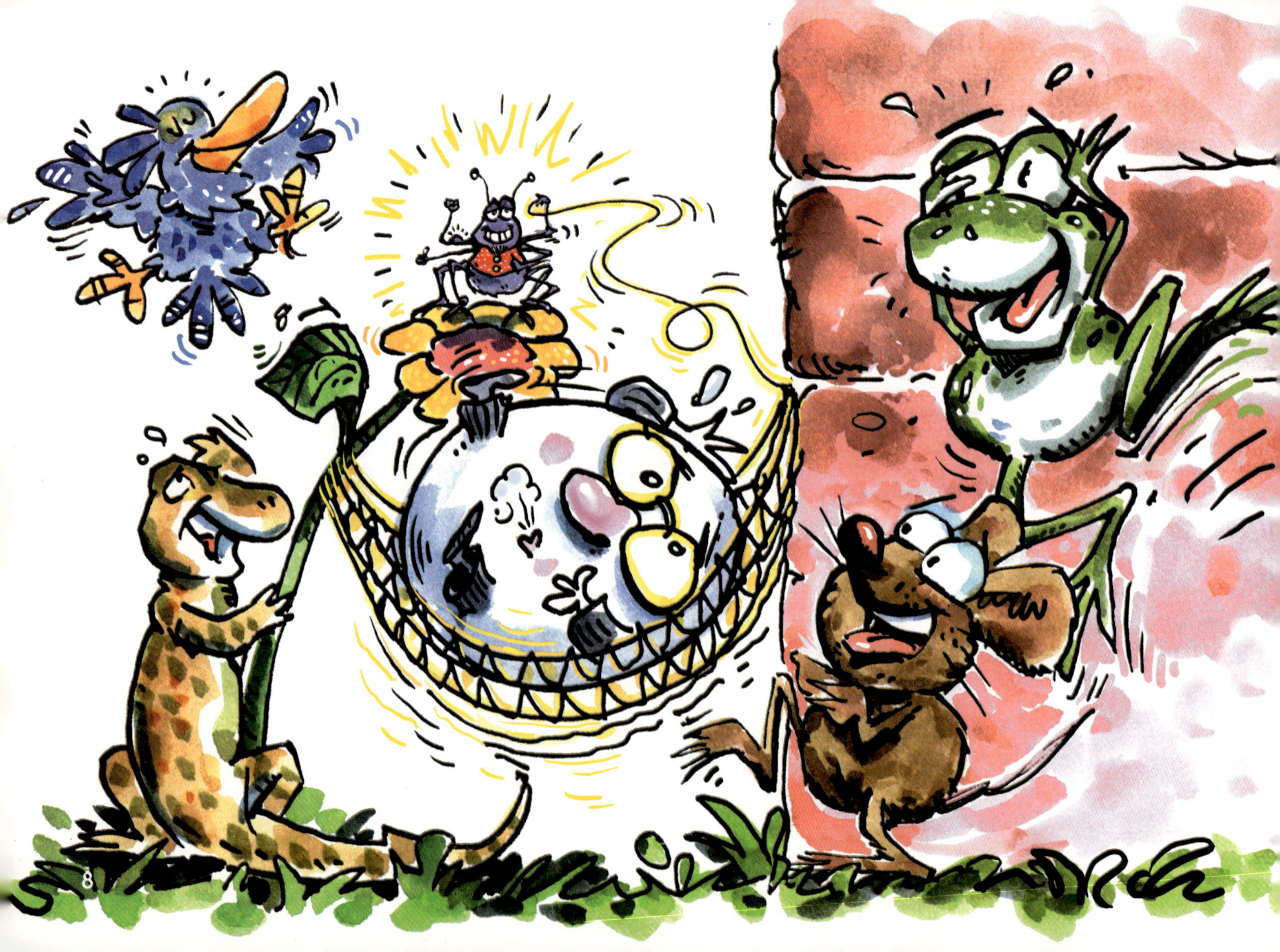